CW00501210

HAMPSTEAD AND HIGHGATE TRAMWAYS

Series editor Robert J Harley

Dave Jones

MP Middleton Press

Cover Picture: The conductor of car 559 stands proudly in front of his charge. Journey time to Moorgate was 33 minutes compared to 37 minutes by today's 214 bus, a descendant of the 15 tram. A steam roller in the background suggests road improvements for the new turning circle of the replacement trolleybuses. The fine St.Albans Villas to the right of the car were destroyed by bombing during World War II. (H.B.Priestley)

Cover Colours: These are similar to the livery employed by the London Street Tramways Company on its vehicles serving the Swains Lane to Holborn route.

First published May 1995

ISBN 1 873793 53 7

© Middleton Press 1995

Design - Deborah Goodridge

Published by Middleton Press
Easebourne Lane
Midhurst
West Sussex
GU29 9AZ
Tel: 01730 813169

Printed & bound by Biddles Ltd,
Guildford and Kings Lynn

CONTENTS

GEOGRAPHICAL SETTING

Some five miles to the north of the City of London and formerly in the county of Middlesex, the two villages, Hampstead and Highgate, stand at the top of a steep hill at some 400 feet above sea level. Set in the Forest of Middlesex, they provided quite an obstacle for the traveller from the south. With the growth of London, which rapidly advanced with the coming of railways and tramways in the mid to late nineteenth century, the gap between London and these villages was soon built over, only Hampstead Heath itself which remains one of North London's largest open spaces keeping the two villages apart.

INTRODUCTION AND ACKNOWLEDGEMENTS

It was with some trepidation that I set out to assemble the photographs that make up this volume in the Tramway Classic series, the first to cover North London beyond the Kingsway Subway. I have always had a keen interest in both the tramways of London generally, and in the history of my particular part of London, Kentish Town. I am sure that I was only one of many people to ask Robert Harley when he was going to bring the series north of the river, and I was talked into making it happen.

I would like to thank the many photographers who took the time and trouble all those years ago to stand by the roadside, and occasionally in the middle of the road, to record this fascinating form of transport. H.B.Priestley, W.A.Camwell and D.W.K. Jones are three names worthy of special mention as they photographed most of the routes covered shortly before they were converted to trolleybus operation in the late thirties. In the heyday of the commercial postcard at the turn of the century there were many publishers offering views of the district, but one in particular stands out above all of the others and that is Charles Martin, and I must thank Gordon Bromberger for allowing me access to his extensive collection. One person who must have walked the whole system many times over during the last couple of years of tramway operation in 1951/52 is John Meredith, whose work will by now be familiar to regular readers of this series. To the many other photographers whose names appear, and to those whose names are not recorded because we don't know who you are, thank you, I have tried to give due credit where it is known.

Much reference was made to volume two of Ted Oakley's excellent and highly recommended history of the LCC Tramways, along with his earlier work with David Willoughby, the London Transport Tramways Handbook. Once again, the drawings of Terry Russell have been used to illustrate the rolling stock section. The staff at Camden Local Studies and Archives Centre at Swiss Cottage Library supplied some new views from their extensive and well organised collection. I received valuable help from Rosemary Thacker and Glynn Wilton during a day spent in the library of The National Tramway Museum at Crich. As a kind of repayment to them, I was part of a team that the previous day had just delivered to the Museum the lower saloon of a new tramcar, London Transport E/1 No 1622. It had been restored in London by the London County Council Tramways Trust, an organisation whose sole aim is the restoration of London trams and which I am privileged to be a part.

Finally thank you to Robert Harley for putting up with my excuses for lack of progress with this volume and for not pushing me too hard while work was going on to finish 1622. Just one more thing, if anyone should notice a preference towards the Parliament Hill services in this volume, this is quite intentional!

HISTORICAL BACKGROUND

The first horse drawn tramways were laid down around 1870, with gradual extension and improvement following during the next few years. The main operating company was the London Street Tramways Co, except for the Upper Street and Holloway Road lines which were run by the North Metropolitan Tramways Co. In 1891 an approach was made by the LCC to take over the London Street Tramway services, and following very long and complicated negotiations, both companies were taken over by the LCC, who at that time had no powers to operate a tramway, so in 1897 the system was leased to the North Met. Co to be operated for the LCC. Further extensions and improvements continued, but now under acts obtained by the LCC.

In 1883 construction of a totally new type of tramway commenced on Highgate Hill. It was to be a 3ft.6ins./1067mm gauge cable hauled line, running from a terminus adjacent to the Archway Tavern, climbing the hill to an upper terminus at the junction of Southwood Lane in the centre of Highgate Village. This was to be the first cable hauled tramway in Europe, and was built using the same principal as that still running today in San Francisco. The line opened in 1884 and despite a number of minor mishaps ran until a somewhat more serious accident occurred in 1892 when the line was closed, not re-opening until April 1897.

By now the horse tramway extensions had reached their limits, the inhabitants of Highgate having a service right into the centre of the village, while following fierce opposition to a proposed line, their neighbours in Hampstead had a service only to the southern edge at South End Green.

In 1906 following the termination of the North Met Co's lease by the LCC, work began on electrifying the existing horse lines using the conduit system of current collection. The first part tackled was a short line from the Angel to the Agricultural Hall in Upper Street, terminating in a double track and lay-by, which survived until the end of tramway operation in 1952. This was extended to Highbury Corner and opened for public service in November 1906. The existing horse car depot at St Pauls Road was modified in order that the single deck subway cars operating the service could be stabled overnight while work was under way

building Holloway depot and the lines that would connect it to the system existing so far. The remainder of the lines were reconstructed in various stages during the next five years, the last of which was to be that along Highgate Road from the Bull and Gate to the Swains Lane terminus which was completed in May 1911. Two lines though were never converted to electric operation, that in Liverpool Road and the southern part of Kentish Town Road, both closing with the cessation of horse traffic. The Highgate Hill cable line had been closed in August 1909, to be rebuilt as a standard gauge electric line, with a specially reinforced conduit for the slipper brakes that were to be fitted to the cars using this line. It was re-opened in March 1910, a remarkably speedy operation.

The Metropolitan Electric Tramways had reached the Archway from the north in mid 1905, where they had to wait until the end of 1914 for the LCC to extend and construct a conduit change pit to allow through services to operate.

The entire system was taken over by the London Passenger Transport Board in July 1933, and they appeared to waste little time in drawing up plans to rid London of its trams. By the end of 1938 all but the three services through the Kingsway Subway and service 11 to Highgate Village had been converted to trolleybus operation, route 11 finally giving way to the 611 in December 1939. Conversion plans were then halted for the duration of the war, but were soon put back into action when peace resumed and things had settled down. In April 1952 services 33 and 35 became the last to run through north London with the closure of the Kingsway Subway. Service 31 had gone in 1950, but by this time trams were replaced by diesel buses whose fuel was much cheaper. The trolleybus too was under threat and the last local trolleybus route ceased in 1961.

As a postscript, in 1994 there were plans being discussed for a new tramway service from Tottenham Court Road to Palmers Green, following the same routes through Camden Town and the Nags Head, along with a branch to Hampstead. We shall have to wait and see, but I doubt that if it ever does happen, they will have the same character as the cars that went before.

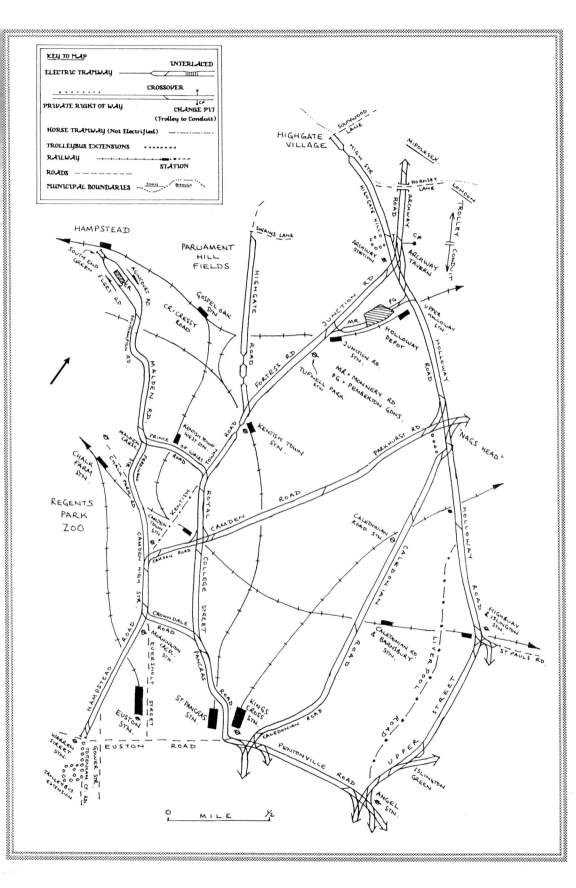

1. We begin at the Hampstead Road terminus where the crew rest inside MET G class car 233 while they await departure time for the long journey back to Barnet. The triangular marking on the dash warns other road users that the car has eight wheel brakes. (R.Elliott)

2. Two class G cars are seen in tandem; they have been fitted with windscreens and are now in the ownership of London Transport. These cars began life in 1909 as 74 seat open toppers, and were fitted with top covers made by the LGOC at their Chiswick works in the late 1920s. Most of the buildings seen here were swept away in the 1960s with the construction of the Euston underpass. (D.Jones Coll.)

3. E/1 car 1053 with a twisted destination blind passes among an assortment of horse and hand propelled traffic in Hampstead Road shortly after leaving the terminus. (Camden Libraries)

Euston Road to Hampstead and Highgate (Horse Traction).

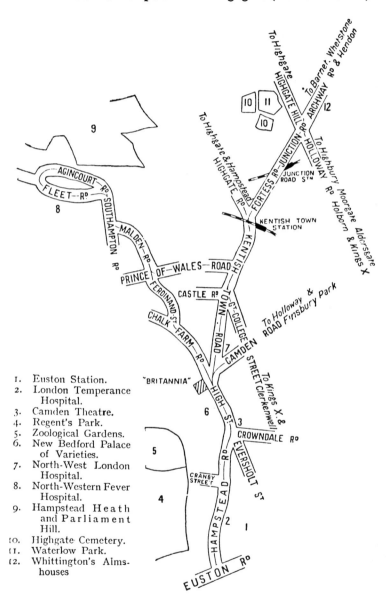

1. Euston Station.
2. London Temperance Hospital.
3. Camden Theatre.
4. Regent's Park.
5. Zoological Gardens.
6. New Bedford Palace of Varieties.
7. North-West London Hospital.
8. North-Western Fever Hospital.
9. Hampstead Heath and Parliament Hill.
10. Highgate Cemetery.
11. Waterlow Park.
12. Whittington's Alms-houses

4. On its way to Hampstead, car 581 pauses at the stop in Crowndale Road before turning right into Camden High Street. This new line connecting Camden High Street with Pancras Road was opened in late 1909, there being no horse car lines along here before. To the left of the picture is the Camden Theatre, for many years used by BBC radio as a recording studio for variety programmes, many of the famous Goon Shows being recorded here. (H.B.Priestley)

5. There must have been something odd about Finsbury Park destination blinds causing them to twist. Here we see car 951 passing the Cobden Statue at the junction of Crowndale Road. Note the Metropolitan Police ambulance station sited by the statue. A wheeled stretcher would be kept here and manned when needed by the nearest available police constable. (Camden Libraries)

6. Car 1066 on its way to Tottenham Court Road passes along Camden High Street and approaches the stop at the corner of Greenland Street. (Camden Libraries)

7. Car 2055 waits in heavy traffic to cross the busy Camden Town junction. This and E/1 car 1268 ahead will turn right into Camden Road and follow the same route as far as Amhurst Park, while the STL motor bus trying to squeeze through on the nearside will go straight ahead, bound for Hampstead. (H.B.Priestley)

8. At the same location, but quite what it is that has the attention of the driver of ex MET class H car 2182, as well as the driver of the following bus we shall probably never know. (H.B.Priestley)

9.   Car 2182 again, but this time heading towards town, is seen turning from Camden Road into Camden High Street. The trams are already being ousted by the trolleybus, service 29 having given way to route 629 in May 1938, while the 27 has until November before it too would be replaced. A fire engine waits among the traffic. (H.B.Priestley)

10. 500 series E/1 car 584 stands at Camden Town while on its way to Moorgate. The presence of an inspector and the conductor at the "front end" suggests that it may have halted before clearing the points and is now "stuck on the dead." Use of the trolleybus overhead in such situations was forbidden, they will have to await the next car to push it clear of the points and back onto a live section. (H.B.Priestley)

11. Lightly loaded E class car 634, dating from 1906, waits for a clear road before crossing the junction. Behind the car is Camden Town underground station, badly damaged during an air raid in 1940. (H.B.Priestley)

12. In pre-World War I, E/1 car 1225 is in Malden Road by the junction with Prince of Wales Road. Note the remains of the horse car track in front of the Mother Shipton public house. These rails remained in place until the early 1950s. (D.Jones Coll.)

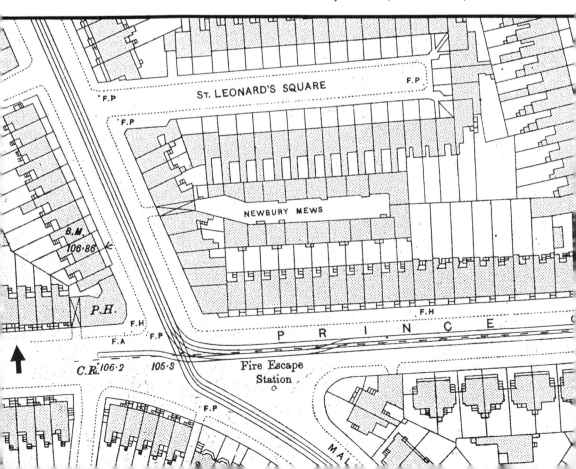

13. In Malden Road, just before the sharp turn at "The Priory", E class cars 726 and 530 pass in opposite directions with the steeple of St. Andrews Church appearing to rise from the roof of car 530! The buildings on the left will soon lose their metal railings as salvage for the war effort. By the late sixties the buildings too will have gone. Span wires have been put up for the trolleybus overhead, but as yet no running wires. (H.B.Priestley)

14. The motorman of car 581 notches up as he pulls away from the stop in Southampton Road, no doubt hoping to stay ahead of the STL on route 24, a bus route little changed in 1995. (H.B.Priestley)

15. The last section before the terminus at Hampstead comprised a single line loop via Fleet Road and Agincourt Road. Here we see E/1 car 534 on its way back to Holborn, about to leave the one-way loop and cross into Southampton Road. It was to be the 1960s before this same one way system was adopted for all traffic. (H.B.Priestley)

16. Hampstead Depot was built during 1913 and with only a handful of cars required to cover the services in the area, there was always plenty of surplus capacity. Initially it had been anticipated that further tramway extensions would take place, but these never came about and it became possible to use this space for storage of surplus and withdrawn cars awaiting disposal, and for a certain amount of local overhaul and painting work. Late in 1994 the depot was demolished to be replaced by housing. (W.A.Camwell)

17. The interior of Hampstead Depot in early 1938 and stored out of service with a damaged dash, car 2272 waits for Nemesis in the form of the scrapman's torch. The more modern Feltham car 2077 has also been damaged in an accident and it will be the last Feltham to be transferred to Telford Avenue Depot, south of the river in Streatham. In 1950 it arrived in Leeds and it was withdrawn from service in 1957. (W.A.Camwell)

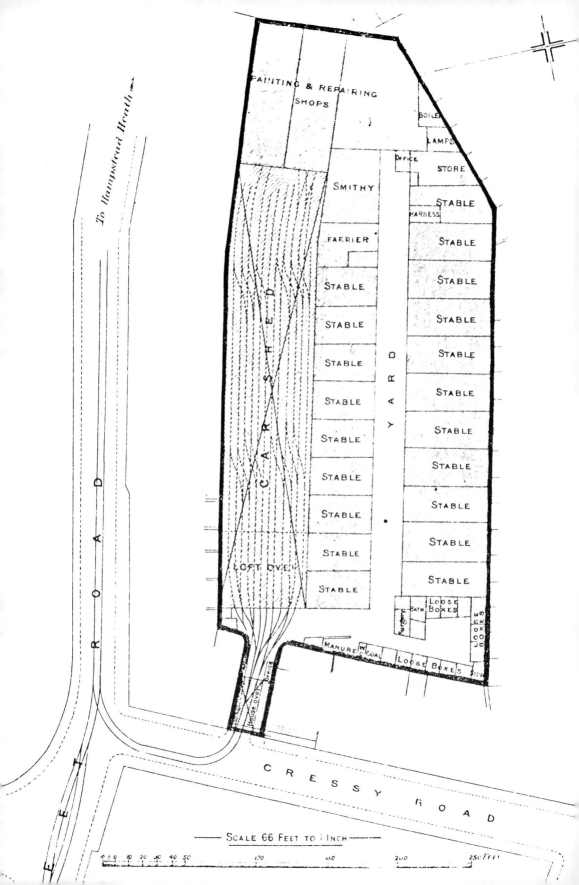

PAINTING & REPAIRING SHOPS

BOILER

LAMPS

OFFICE

STORE

SMITHY

STABLE

HARNESS

FARRIER

STABLE

STABLE

STABLE

STABLE

STABLE

STABLE

STABLE

STABLE

STABLE

STABLE

STABLE

STABLE

STABLE

STABLE

STABLE

STABLE

STABLE

STABLE

STABLE

STABLE

STABLE

LOFT OVER

STABLE

STABLE

LOOSE BOXES

BATH

LOOSE BOXES

MANURE

COAL

LOOSE BOXES

HOUSE OVER

OFFICE

CAR SHED

YARD

To Hampstead Heath

R O A D

F E E T

C R E S S Y   R O A D

SCALE 66 FEET TO 1 INCH

10 5 0   10   20   30   40   50   100   150   200   250 FEET

18. Here in 1946 we see a group of rather sorry looking trams, stored for the duration of the war. A few did see further use, but the majority were either scrapped on site or sold. All have white painted fenders to show that they had seen some use during the very early days of the war. (J.H.Meredith)

19. In 1947 at the depot entrance is the body of E/1 car 1607, stripped of its trucks and other running gear, but still with wartime blast netting at the windows. It has been loaded onto a road trailer before being taken off to start a new, albeit short life. This was one of at least five cars that saw use as holiday homes on Hayling Island. One of these cars, 1622, was recovered in 1980 by the London County Council Tramways Trust for restoration and eventual operation at the National Tramway Museum at Crich, Derbyshire. (D.Jones Coll.)

20. At the top end of Fleet Road car 531 stands
awaiting space before moving across to the
double tracked terminus at South End Green.
Notice the brand new bowstring traction
standards which have been erected for the new
trolleybuses. (A.B.Cross)

21. A busy scene as North Metropolitan horse
cars manoeuvre around the terminus. This is
still a well used bus terminus today, and is
surprisingly little altered. (D.Jones Coll.)

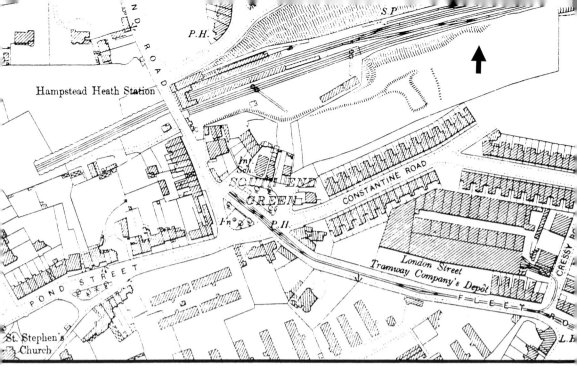

22. Car 552 arrives from Holborn while two E class trams are waiting to depart. All three cars carry their own funeral notice on the rocker panels announcing that within a few days there will be a new trolleybus service. (D.W.K.Jones)

LONDON'S TRAMWAYS

HAMPSTEAD HEATH
AND KEN WOOD

SERVICES	FROM	VIA
3·7	HOLBORN	KINGS CROSS
5·15	MOORGATE	CITY ROAD AND KINGS CROSS
11	MOORGATE	HOLLOWAY ROAD
25	TOTTENHAM CT. RD.	

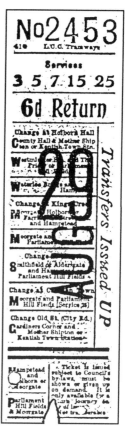

No 2453
41⊙ L.U.C. Tramways
Services
3 5 7 15 25
6d Return

29 AUG

Transfers Isssued Up

23. The crew have their photograph taken on the front platform of E/1 car 1125. This was shortly after the introduction of electric services in late 1909. Service numbers were not introduced until the beginning of 1913, when the Hampstead to Tottenham Court Road route was given the number 1. (Camden Libraries)

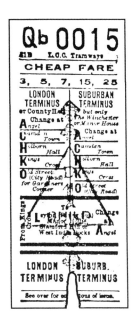

24. A final look at the South End Green terminus on what looks as if it might have been August Bank Holiday, judging by the rain! The drivers will hardly be entering into the spirit of "Appy Ampstead." (D.Jones Coll.)

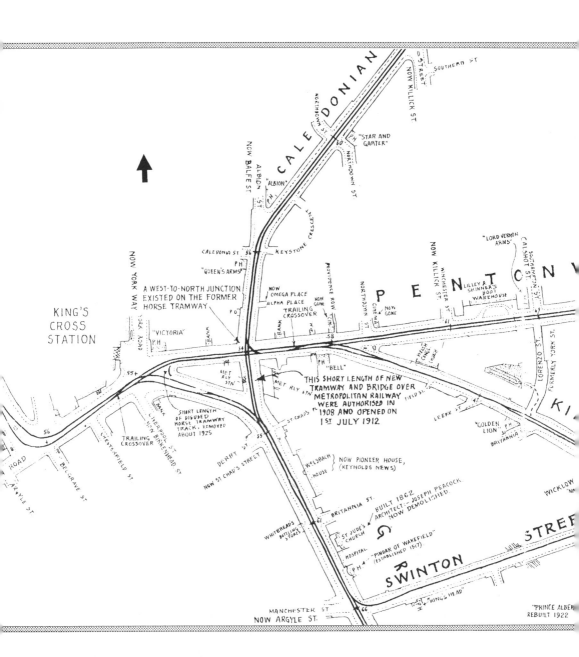

25. During the re-siting of the Metropolitan Line station there was severe disruption to road traffic around Kings Cross Station while massive girders were lowered into position over the running tunnels to support the road above. Here car 634 passes through the site, before turning right into Pancras Road and heading towards Hampstead. (H.B.Priestley)

26. Passengers climb the steps on to a Hampstead bound tram in Pancras Road. Behind is the curved facade of the Great Northern Hotel, built in 1851 and following the line of the original roadway here. (H.B.Priestley)

27. A horse car on the Swains Lane to Moorgate service enters Pancras Road from Great College Street. Note that there was no tramway at this time in Crowndale Road. The College Arms in the background takes its name from the Veterinary College opposite, which still occupies the site, although much rebuilt. The drinking fountain on the pavement is one of many of this type seen around the borough. (G.Bromberger Coll.)

28. At much the same point as the previous view, but some thirty years later in 1938, car 726 enters Crowndale Road. On the left is the old St Pancras Town Hall built in 1840 and replaced in 1937 by the new building in Euston Road. (H.B.Priestley)

29. Passing under the North London Railway bridge in Kentish Town Road is a northbound horse car. This tram route was never converted to electric operation largely due to the lack of expected traffic, coupled with the very tight clearance under the bridge. Another scene that has changed little. (G.Bromberger Coll.)

Notice to Drivers and Conductors.

The method of operating the points at this junction will be revised on and from Wednesday 8th July, 1936. The
Driver will pull the points from the new socket which has been fitted between the two tracks as follows :—

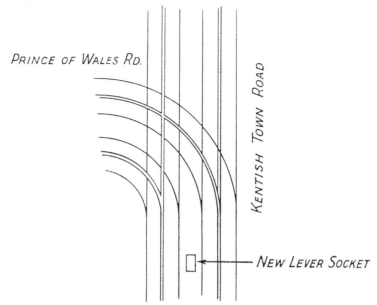

30. June 1938 and an almost full car loads yet more in Kentish Town Road at the Prince of Wales Road stop; cars for Hampstead would turn left here. The model yacht will no doubt soon be launched into Highgate Pond, a short walk from the Swains Lane terminus. (H.B.Priestley)

Holborn to Hampstead and Highgate (Swain's Lane).
(Horse and Electric Traction.)

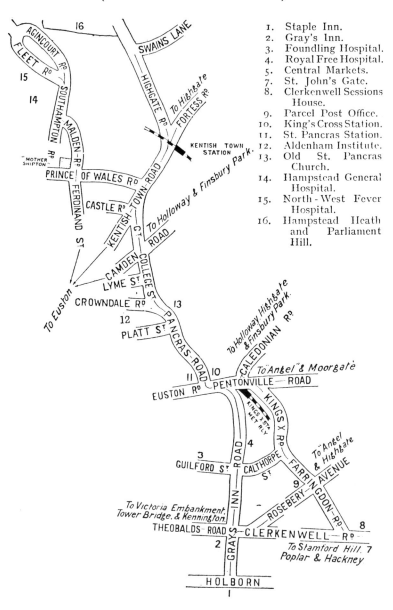

1. Staple Inn.
2. Gray's Inn.
3. Foundling Hospital.
4. Royal Free Hospital.
5. Central Markets.
7. St. John's Gate.
8. Clerkenwell Sessions House.
9. Parcel Post Office.
10. King's Cross Station.
11. St. Pancras Station.
12. Aldenham Institute.
13. Old St. Pancras Church.
14. Hampstead General Hospital.
15. North - West Fever Hospital.
16. Hampstead Heath and Parliament Hill.

31. With the North London Drapery Stores being rebuilt ahead, car 608 from Hampstead waits to turn from Prince of Wales Road into Kentish Town Road for the run to Holborn. (H.B.Priestley)

32. In Prince of Wales Road a horse car has just passed beneath the low arch of the North London Railway at Kentish Town station (renamed Kentish Town West in 1924). The lack of headroom continues to be a problem here. On the right at the corner of Raydon Street is the Governesses Benevolent Institute of 1849, later becoming temporary home to a number of schools, a purpose which it still serves today. (D.Jones Coll.)

33. Approaching the single line section near Kentish Town Underground Station, E class car 537 on service 15 passes the narrow entrance to Holmes Road. The site of Burtons, the well known gents outfitters is now McDonalds, the equally well known fast food chain. (D.Jones Coll.)

34. On the single line just north of the previous view, car 520 heads south. The buildings to the right were soon to be demolished and following a slight widening of the roadway, were eventually replaced by modern shops and a library. But where have all the shoppers gone? (H.B.Priestley)

35. Between the underground station and the Assembly House is Kentish Town Midland Railway station. A hoarding invites passengers to travel to either Birmingham or Dudley Port for only six shillings and sixpence (32p) return as a Holborn bound car approaches. (D.Jones Coll.)

910.—CONVERSION TO TROLLEYBUS OPERATION OF ROUTES Nos. 3, 5, 7 AND 15.

Notice to Inspectors and Conductors.

On Sunday, 10th July, 1938, Tram Routes Nos. 3, 5, 7 and 15 will be converted to trolleybus operation shewn :—

Tram Route No.	Trolleybus Route No.	Route.	Remarks.
3	513	Hampstead and Holborn/Farringdon Street Loop via Grays Inn Road	Hampstead Depot will be closed and trolleybuses will operate these services from Holloway Depot.
7	613	Parliament Hill Fields and Farringdon Street/Holborn Loop via Farringdon Road	
5	639	Hampstead and Moorgate (Finsbury Square)	
15	615	Parliament Hill Fields and Moorgate (Finsbury Square)	

Route Numbers.

Route No. 513 will be shewn on trolleybuses leaving Hampstead and will be retained until arriving back at Parliament Hill Fields.   Route No. 613 will be shewn on trolleybuses leaving Parliament Hill Fields and will be retained until arriving back at Hampstead.

36. Entering Highgate Road towards "The Fields", car 538 pauses at the stop. To the right is Fortess Road with lines of sentry like traction poles to support the new trolleybus overhead wires. (H.B.Priestley)

37. Long after the closure of the services through Kentish Town, a single line was kept open to transfer trams between Hampstead and Holloway depots and on to the rest of the system. This is Junction Road close to Monnery Road in July 1952. The Express Dairy milk float provides the only electric traction in this view. (J.C.Gillham)

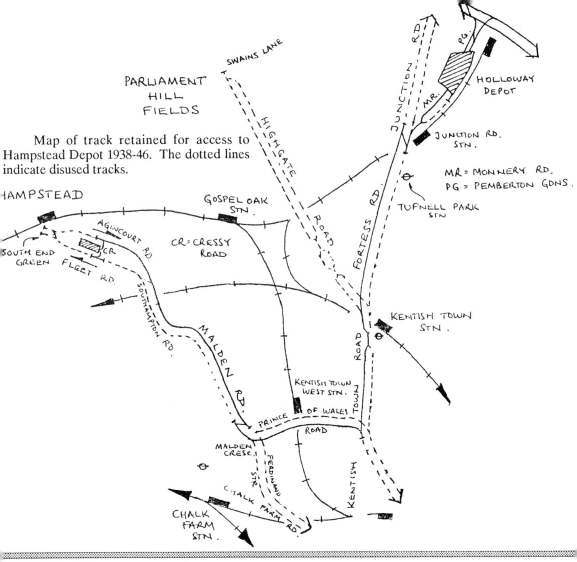

PARLIAMENT
HILL
FIELDS

SWAINS LANE

HIGHGATE

Map of track retained for access to
Hampstead Depot 1938-46. The dotted lines
indicate disused tracks.

HOLLOWAY
DEPOT

JUNCTION RD.
STN.

MR = MONNERY RD.
PG = PEMBERTON GDNS.

TUFNELL PARK
STN

HAMPSTEAD

GOSPEL OAK
STN.

AGINCOURT RD.

CR = CRESSY
ROAD

SOUTH END
GREEN

FLEET RD.

CR

SOUTHAMPTON RD.

ROAD

FORTESS RD.

KENTISH TOWN
STN.

MALDEN RD.

ROAD

KENTISH TOWN
WEST STN.

OF WALES

KENTISH TOWN

PRINCE

ROAD

MALDEN
CRESC.

FERDINAND STR.

CHALK FARM RD.

KENTISH

CHALK
FARM
STN.

38. In Junction Road a horse car nears the end
of its journey to the Archway. It has just passed
the entrance to the depot near Poynings Road.
This depot, complete with most of the track
survived until the 1960s when housing was put
up on the site. It is still possible to trace the
position of the stables today.
(G.Bromberger Coll.)

39. Back in Highgate Road we see one of the many passing loops that were a feature here in horse car days; this one is just north of Lady Somerset Road. The bridge in the distance carries the Tottenham & Hampstead Junction Railway and was of insufficient clearance when top covered electric cars were introduced. The LCC had to lower the roadway at great expense to create the extra headroom. The horse trams carried enamel notices requesting upper deck passengers to remain seated when passing under the bridge. The canopies of Highgate Road Station may just be seen at either end of the bridge. (G.Bromberger Coll.)

40. A well loaded horse car climbs away from the junction of Gordon House Road and Chetwynd Road on the last leg of its journey. Today traffic lights control this busy cross roads. (D.Jones Coll.)

41. Two very new electric cars pass just fifty yards further on from the previous picture. A group of children heads towards a picnic in "The Fields" on this sunny summer's day. (D.Jones Coll.)

42. The same viewpoint in the early thirties and we witness the arrival of car 565. The trees in front of Grove Terrace have been heavily cut back, giving a rare view of this fine row of late 18th century buildings. (D.Jones Coll.)

285.—HIGHGATE ROAD TERMINUS.

Notice to Motormen and Conductors.

On and after Monday, 7th May, 1934, the following instructions must be strictly observed :—

No car is to stand on the single line.

After discharging passengers at the shelter as at present, cars are to cross over to the up track—the leading car to wait with the buffer opposite the lamp post at the corner of St. Alban's Road.

43. In red LCC livery, car 571 stands at Parliament Hill Fields terminus. The LCC waiting room just visible to the left of the tram was built on land within Parliament Hill Fields. (D.Jones Coll.)

44. The date is 10th April 1938 and an animated scene at Swains Lane terminus is caught in time. The motorman keeps an wary eye out for the service 7 tram which is about to reverse. The conductor and the couple about to pass behind car 543 seem more interested in the photographer. (W.A.Camwell)

45. A last look at the tree lined Highgate
Road, with E class car 530 waiting to pull
forward to the crossover. Behind the trees
stands Parliament Hill, also known as Kite Hill.
It was from here in 1605 that Guy Fawkes &
Co had planned to watch their own special
firework display as they attempted to blow up
the Houses of Parliament.
(A.D.Packer Coll.)

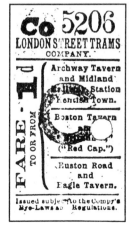

3. CAMDEN TOWN TO NAGS HEAD
VIA CAMDEN & PARKHURST ROADS

46. This is Camden Town Station, better known locally as the "North London." The car nearest the camera will turn left at the bridge towards Kentish Town and the Archway. The station was later renamed Camden Road following the opening of the nearby underground railway. (G.Bromberger Coll.)

47. The driver of MET car 268 notices the photographer as he passes along Camden Road near Rochester Road working on service 27 to Edmonton Depot.
(A.W.V.Mace/ National Tramway Museum)

48. At the "summit" of Camden Road, by the Brecknock Arms public house, a MET class C car on service 31 stops to unload as a model T Ford waits for a clear road before passing the tram on the nearside. In 1843 this was the site of the last fatal duel in England, although some of today's motorists appear to want to continue the tradition. (D.Jones Coll.)

49. E/1 car 1070 on service 31 picks up passengers at the Athenaeum in Parkhurst Road, with Camden Road totally deserted as far as can be seen. A filling station now stands on the site of the Athenaeum. The iron gate to the left leads to Holloway Prison. (D.Jones Coll.)

50. A Feltham car on the Enfield service waits in Parkhurst Road shortly after take over by London Transport. It will soon cross over the Nags Head junction. Note the tram stop sign hanging from a lamp standard on the traffic island. (D.Jones Coll.)

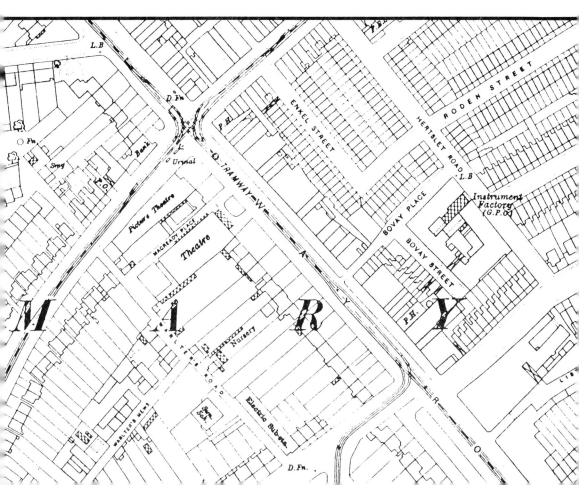

51. The photographer has somehow managed to amuse the crew of car 2203 as well as the passengers in the back of the coach. Working only to Tramway Avenue Edmonton, this may be the crew's last trip of the day so they have every reason to be happy. (H.B.Priestley)

4. KINGS CROSS TO NAGS HEAD
VIA CALEDONIAN ROAD

52. An ex-MET car stands by the Kings Cross Cinema in New Bridge Street. Specially constructed to carry the new electric trams across the Metropolitan Railway, it was opened in 1912 and was at that time adjacent to the station entrance. The inspector appears to be waiting to have a word with someone! (D.Jones Coll.)

53. A group of youngsters has gathered in Caledonian Road close to Lofting Road to watch the photographer, but some are more interested in the novelty of the tramcar. (D .Jones Coll.)

54. Car 2170 is in Camden Road having just turned from Holloway Road and is about to turn left in to Caledonian Road. A board opposite advises that volunteers may enrol for the ARP, a sign of changing times not too far away. (H.B.Priestley)

55. An un-screened ex-MET car lines up behind a new trolleybus waiting to turn into Holloway Road. Note the fully dropped upper deck windows, fitted with safety rails. The date is July 1938 and this service will also fall to the trolleybus before too long. (H.B.Priestley)

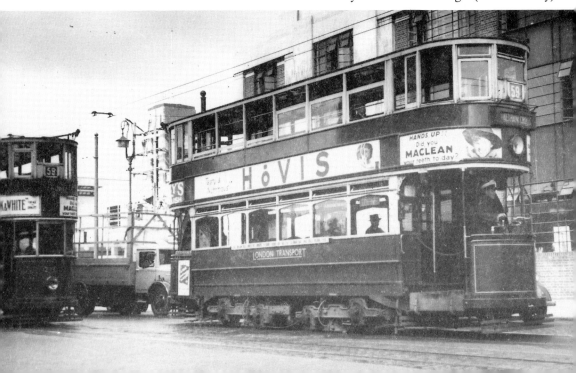

5. KINGS CROSS TO HIGHGATE VILLAGE
VIA ANGEL & HIGHBURY CORNER

56. An E/1 makes the turn from Pentonville Road in to Caledonian Road, heading for the Archway. The car behind on service 5 will go straight ahead and past the front of Kings Cross Station before making its right turn into Pancras Road towards Hampstead. (A.D.Packer Coll.)

57. Climbing Pentonville Road towards Penton Street is E class car 743, bound for Moorgate Street. It was from this point, but looking back down the hill, that John O'Connor painted his famous 1884 view of St Pancras Station complete with horse trams. (National Tramway Museum)

58. At the Angel, and the driver of car 544 was probably not best pleased at having to stop right where he did, it has left him stranded "on the dead." The conductor looks along City Road waiting for the next car along and hoping for a push back on to a live section. (A.D. Packer Coll.)

Q 7377
THE HIGHGATE HILL TRAMWAYS, LIMITED.

1 D

ARCHWAY
TAVERN
to
HIGHGATE.

HIGHGATE
to
ARCHWAY
TAVERN.

C.A.S. Pun & Ticket Co., Ltd., Queen's Rd., Dalston, N.E.

JE 0431
UP L.C.C. Trams. DOWN

Nag's Head
Holloway   D.   Enfield

4

Camden   as   Church
Town Stn.   S. Stephen's

Cobden   Dragon Lne
Statue   Green

...ston   Eaton Park
...oad   Road

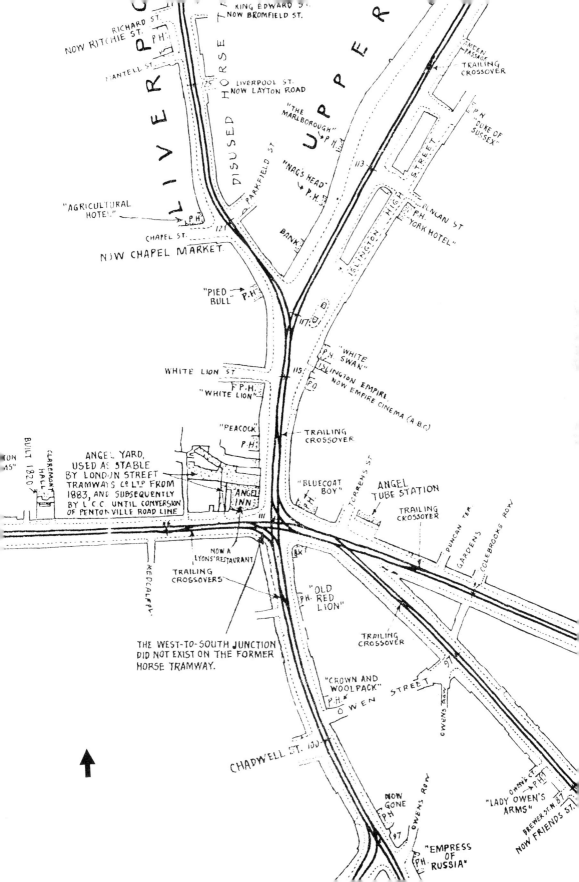

LIVER P

UPPER R

NOW RITCHIE ST.
RICHARD ST.
MANTELL ST.
KING EDWARD S.
NOW BROMFIELD ST.
CAMDEN PASSAGE
TRAILING CROSSOVER

DISUSED HORSE T.

LIVERPOOL ST.
NOW LAYTON ROAD

F.P.N.
"DUKE OF SUSSEX"

"THE MARLBOROUGH" P.H.

113

"NAG'S HEAD" P.H.

PARKFIELD ST.

ISLINGTON HIGH ST.

DUNCAN ST.

P.H. "YORK HOTEL"

"AGRICULTURAL HOTEL"

P.H.

121
CHAPEL ST.

BANK

NEW CHAPEL MARKET

"PIED BULL" P.H.

INT.

WHITE LION ST.

115

"WHITE SWAN" P.H.
ISLINGTON EMPIRE NOW EMPIRE CINEMA (A.B.C.)
F.O.

F.P.H. "WHITE LION"

"PEACOCK" P.H.

TRAILING CROSSOVER

BUILT 1820
CLAREMONT HALL

ANGEL YARD, USED AS STABLE BY LONDON STREET TRAMWAYS Cᵒ LTᴰ FROM 1883, AND SUBSEQUENTLY BY L C C UNTIL CONVERSION OF PENTONVILLE ROAD LINE

"BLUECOAT BOY"

TORRENS ST.

ANGEL TUBE STATION

TRAILING CROSSOVER

DUNCAN TER.
GARDENS
COLEBROOKS ROW

"ANGEL INN"

111

NOW A LYONS' RESTAURANT

TRAILING CROSSOVERS

METCALFE ST.

"OLD P.H. RED LION"

TRAILING CROSSOVER

THE WEST-TO-SOUTH JUNCTION DID NOT EXIST ON THE FORMER HORSE TRAMWAY.

97

"CROWN AND WOOLPACK" P.H.

OWEN STREET

97

OWEN'S ROW

CHADWELL ST. 100

NOW GONE PH.

OWEN'S ROW

"LADY OWEN'S ARMS"

OWEN'S CT. P.H.

BREWER ST. 87
NOW FRIENDS ST.

"EMPRESS OF RUSSIA" PH.

59. Looking from St. John Street at a very busy Angel, MET class H car 260 has cleared the junction, while an LCC single decker heads for the Kingsway Subway. Although every tram would normally carry a spare plough, just in case of trouble, spares would be left at various points along the route. Here two can be seen propped against the feeder pillar on the centre island. (D.Jones Coll.)

60. The same view about thirty years later, January 1952, and an E/3 waits to cross into High Street. Traffic lights have replaced the previous "free for all", and Haig whisky adorns the front of what had been Lockwood and Bradley, "London's Leading Tailors." (R.J.S.Wiseman)

61. In this 1932 view at the crossover between the Angel and Liverpool Road, the conductor of MET class G car 225 has had his attention attracted by something or someone in the bus alongside. In front is an LCC E/1 on service 81 to Bloomsbury, which in turn is headed by a new E/3 on service 35 which will soon pass through the newly reconstructed Kingsway Subway. (G.N.Southerden)

62. Car 170 passes the hoarding covered facade of the Empire Arcade in Upper Street. Today this whole area is a popular venue for antique dealers who have even taken over the adjacent LCC Tramway sub-station. (C.Carter)

63. On 7th April 1951 car 1 was hired for one of its many special tours. The conductor is seen here holding the points for it to reverse at the Charlton Place crossover in Upper Street. This car is in the collection of the National Tramway Museum at Crich. To the left can be seen part of the Royal Agricultural Hall, opened in 1862 and host to various trade shows and entertainments; it was home of tramway trade exhibitions at the beginning of the century. (J.H.Meredith)

64. Sir Hugh Myddleton, who in the early 17th century provided North London with a reliable water supply via his New River, surveys the scene from his pedestal, as car 2003 emerges from Essex Road having come from Manor House. (D.Jones Coll.)

Moorgate, Aldersgate and Holborn to Highgate and Finsbury Park; and Moorgate to King's Cross (Horse and Electric Traction).

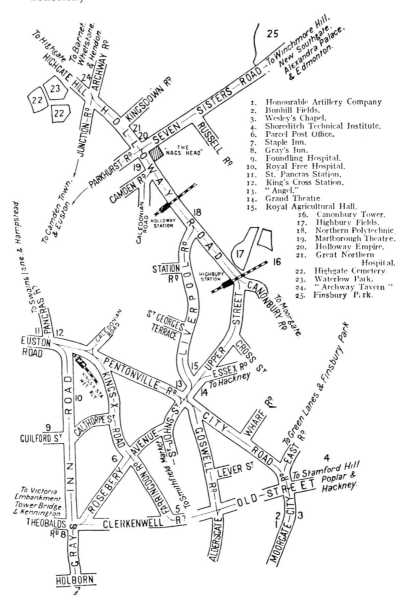

1. Honourable Artillery Company
2. Bunhill Fields.
3. Wesley's Chapel.
4. Shoreditch Technical Institute.
6. Parcel Post Office.
7. Staple Inn.
8. Gray's Inn.
9. Foundling Hospital.
10. Royal Free Hospital.
11. St. Pancras Station.
12. King's Cross Station.
13. "Angel."
14. Grand Theatre.
15. Royal Agricultural Hall.
16. Canonbury Tower.
17. Highbury Fields.
18. Northern Polytechnic.
19. Marlborough Theatre.
20. Holloway Empire.
21. Great Northern Hospital.
22. Highgate Cemetery.
23. Waterlow Park.
24. "Archway Tavern"
25. Finsbury Park.

65. A group of officials remove a damaged plough from an inspection hatch on the three-track section in Upper Street in March 1952. The crews look on no doubt offering "useful" suggestions. The plough has come from car 1921 in the background. (J.H.Meredith)

66. The disabled car 1921 is now to be pushed back to Holloway depot by 175K, one of the Karrier breakdown tenders inherited from the LCC. These sturdy vehicles, packed with equipment for all sorts of emergencies, would turn up at the scene of an incident where the crew would efficiently get the service running again as quickly as possible. It was of good fortune that John Meredith happened to be there to record this particular event. (J.H.Meredith)

67. In December 1939 service 31 was cut back from its Hackney terminus and would for the remainder of its days reverse at Islington, Agricultural Hall. Here in 1950, car 1945 enters the siding while the conductor with his ticket box under his arm rushes off to collect that most essential item, a jug full of tea. (D.W.K.Jones)

68. Crews have a rare moment to pass the time of day as a line of cars are held up near Cross Street. The reason for the delay is the damaged plough on car 1921 illustrated earlier. Just visible at the extreme left is the Odeon Cinema at the corner of Florence Street, built on the site of the former Town Hall, but now serving the motorist as is a filling station. (J.H.Meredith)

69. 1906 - built E class car 734 passes the LCC Fire Brigade Station in this pre-World War I view. The fire appliances at this time were still horse drawn, and would remain so until the early 1920s. A modern fire station now occupies the site. (D.Jones Coll.)

70. Approaching Park Street is car 872 bound for Highgate. To the right, a line of sandwich board men convey their messages while the public around seem not to take much notice. (D.Jones Coll.)

71. Having just turned into Upper Street, a horse car on the Highgate to Moorgate service stands by the Cock Tavern. (D .Jones Coll.)

72. Car 182 has just turned from Holloway Road into Upper Street and is passing a parked Morris Telephone van, forerunner of today's BT vans which are seen just about everywhere! (J.H.Meredith)

73. Outnumbered by trolleybuses, car 1948 makes its way from Holloway Depot to Agricultural Hall, where it will take up service 33. It is March 1952 and within a few weeks this service will be replaced, but by motor buses rather than trolleybuses. (A.D.Packer)

74. A car on the Liverpool Road line prepares to leave Holloway Road for the Angel. This short line survived as a horse drawn tramway until 1913 when it was abandoned. Conversion to electric operation was not considered economic. (D.Jones Coll.)

75. Snowbroom 037, apparently abandoned by its crew, stands beneath the bridge carrying the Great Northern Main Line from Kings Cross over Holloway Road. Converted from former passenger cars in the late twenties, the snowbrooms were used to keep the tracks clear for the running fleet. With no protection for the crew it must have been an unenviable job in the worst weather. The conductor of the following car peers forward as if to see if there is any sign of life. (D.Jones Coll.)

76. Mixed horse drawn and electric working lasted for some time during the reconstruction of the tramways by the LCC. Here, a horse car on the Nags Head to Holborn service reverses to start the journey back to the city, while a Highgate bound electric car waits for a clear line. (C.Carter)

77. In this early 1950s view, car 1980 provides the only remaining tram service through this area. Another ten years and the trolleybus will also be a thing of the past. (C.Carter)

78. A Moorgate bound HR2 pauses at the Nags Head to let to let a Waltham Cross bound car on service 79 make the right turn into Seven Sisters Road. A couple of intending passengers are preparing to board the moving car. (A.D.Packer Coll.)

79. A motorcyclist carefully picks his way across the tracks, which combined with wood blocks and granite setts can make for a very slippery road surface. A Highgate Village bound tram heads a line of cars on this very busy day. (D.Jones Coll.)

80. The same spot, but now with the Parkhurst Road to Seven Sisters Road tracks removed, car 1944 crosses under a vast array of trolley-bus overhead at what became London's busiest trolleybus junction. In the background can be seen the Marlborough Theatre, opened in 1903 and finally closing its doors in 1957, by which time it had become a cinema. Another theatre, The Parkhurst, had occupied the site of Holloway Arcade until 1930. (London Trolleybus Preservation Society)

81. A horse car passes the Great Northern Hospital, later to become the Royal Northern, and much enlarged in the 1960s but now a victim of health cuts, closed and boarded up. (D.Jones Coll.)

82. Stopping to let passengers alight is car 140. The scene is just below Pemberton Gardens where the tracks to Holloway Depot branched off to the left. Hardly at any time of day or night nowadays is Holloway Road as free of traffic as this. (H.B.Priestley)

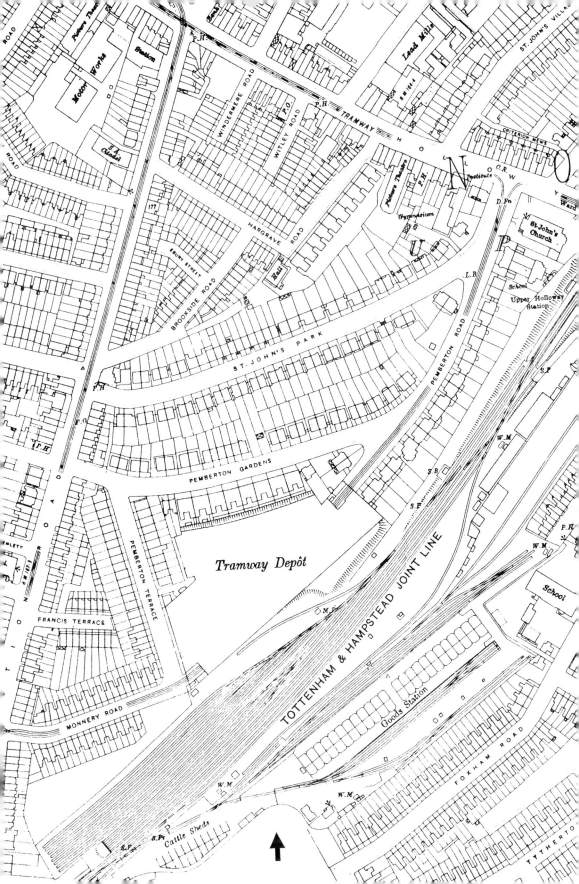

83. Car 185 turns from Pemberton Gardens to make the short journey to the Archway where it will pick up passengers ready to depart for Forest Hill far away in that great unknown, South London. A breakdown tender is parked at the corner ready to deal with any emergency on the road. (D.Jones Coll.)

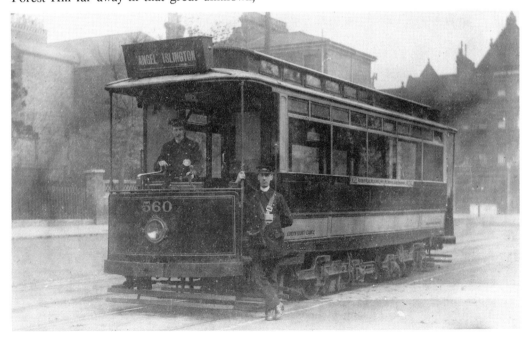

84. The local photographer evidently did a good trade just here as there are many views of crews posing with their cars. Here we see car 560, an F class tram built for operation through the Kingsway Subway. (D.Jones Coll.)

85. E class car 745 is photographed before setting out on a workmans journey, usually a very early morning duty. (D.Jones Coll.)

86. Car 1156 enters the depot after finishing a turn on service 41, Moorgate to Manor House. A solitary motor car is parked in Pemberton Gardens where now there would be a continuous line of such vehicles belonging to residents and bus garage staff. (A.B.Cross)

87. Looking spick and span after its encounter with the car washer at Holloway Depot, car 1046 is ready for the road. In those days public service vehicles were regularly cleaned. (LCC official photo)

88. A 1950s view inside the depot shows tram, trolleybus and bus. Only a few roads retained the service pits after conversion for trolleybus operation. In its busiest period this depot was capable of housing over 300 cars. The wooden shuttering designed to protect maintenance staff from the exposed current rails is well illustrated here. The traverser pit, which ran the full width of the depot, is visible in the centre of the view. (D.W.K.Jones)

89. Four-wheel M class car 1440 stands in Monnery Road. (D.Jones Coll.)

90. On 5th April 1952, the last day of the Kingsway Subway services, E/3 car 184 passes over the pointwork at Pemberton Gardens and continues the short distance to the Archway junction where it will terminate. (J.H.Meredith)

91. Disabled car 1921, last seen being pushed away from Upper Street by the Karrier breakdown tender, is here being "walked" wrong line along Holloway Road just north of Pemberton Gardens, taking power from the trolleybus overhead. After turning the corner it will cross over and regain the correct line and continue to the depot by this method. (D.Jones Coll.)

92.   Running in to Holloway Depot from service 27, car 1157 waits for traffic to clear before reversing from Holloway Road into Pemberton Gardens.   (H.B.Priestley)

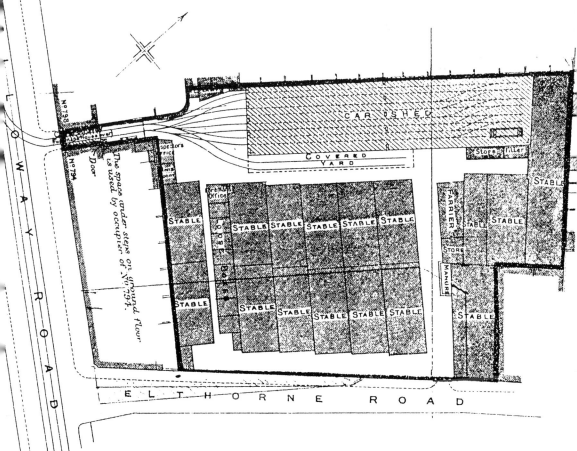

93. Just north of Elthorne Road was a depot of The North Metropolitan Tramways Co.; the entrance is seen here with the surviving horse car tracks in 1953. Amazingly this track has survived much development in the area and could still be seen in 1995 although the depot itself has been demolished. (J.C.Gillham)

94. Just like today's buses, after waiting for an age along come three at once! Cars 187, 1907 and 160 are at the Archway junction in Holloway Road; the facing crossover can be seen here. Car 160 was planned to be an HR2, but the equal wheel trucks were used for experimental car 1; 160 subsequently acquired a spare pair of maximum traction trucks, becoming the only trolleyless E/3. (J.H.Meredith)

OS map at 50" to 1 mile of Archway Tavern

95. The Archway Tavern was recorded in horse car days with a car on the Archway to Euston service just arriving. Visible here is the single line stub in Archway Road with a double line in Highgate Hill, facing on to the 3ft.6ins. gauge tracks of the cable hauled tramway. Sidings were located in front of the tavern for the storage of trams. (D.Jones Coll.)

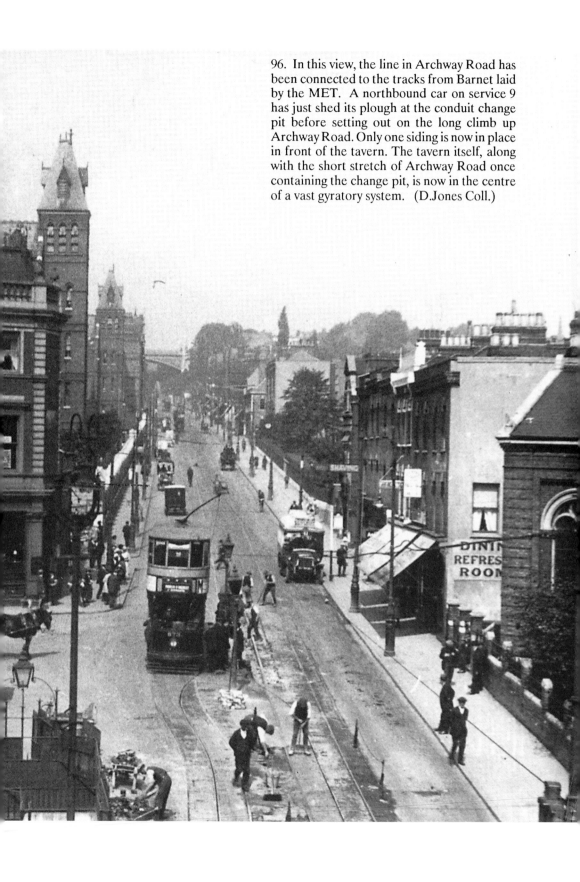

96. In this view, the line in Archway Road has been connected to the tracks from Barnet laid by the MET. A northbound car on service 9 has just shed its plough at the conduit change pit before setting out on the long climb up Archway Road. Only one siding is now in place in front of the tavern. The tavern itself, along with the short stretch of Archway Road once containing the change pit, is now in the centre of a vast gyratory system. (D.Jones Coll.)

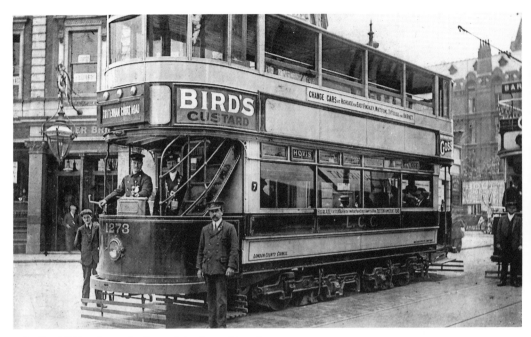

97. Car 1273 waits at the foot of Archway Road while the crew and an inspector have their photograph taken. The upper deck drop windows are fully opened suggesting very warm weather. (A.D.Packer Coll.)

98. Car 2252 prepares to cross the maze of tracks into Junction Road having just picked up its plough at the change pit. Gravity will help it across the many dead sections in the conduit where the tracks cross each other. (H.B.Priestley)

99. Car 880 has just shed its plough, the trolley has been put on the wire, the rope has been wound into the pig-tail and is being stowed by an inspector before the car sets off. The plough fork can be seen lying in the road to the right of the car, this is used for guiding the plough into the carriers of town bound trams. (H.B.Priestley)

100. The Highgate Archway was opened to the public on 21st August 1813. In 1897 the old archway was replaced by the iron bridge depicted in this view. Note MET car 93 gliding up the hill on its way to Barnet. (R.J.Harley Coll.)

101. A youthful passenger boards an HR2 on
a short working of service 11, running as an
extra to Essex Road. To the left, parked on the
site of the former siding, is an elderly NS type
bus now relegated to a staff canteen.
(H.B.Priestley)

102. Just arrived from Farringdon Street is car
852 which will take its rest here before setting
off again on the return journey. To the left can
be seen Highgate Underground Station, later
to be renamed Archway on the Barnet branch
of the Northern Line.   (D.Jones Coll.)

103. On 29th March 1952, just a few days before the last trams were to run in this area, car 186 stands in Highgate Hill, the roadway covered in snow. With tracks soon becoming covered by snow and slush, a drivers knowledge of the exact whereabouts of crossovers and dead sections would be essential. (J.C.Gillham)

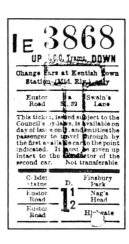

LONDON COUNTY COUNCIL TRAMWAYS

Service Nos. 9 & 11

MOORGATE AND HIGH BARNET
MOORGATE AND HIGHGATE VILLAGE

Revised $\frac{1}{2}^{d}$ Fare Stages as under are now in operation:—

Moorgate	—	—	—	— Old Street
Old Street	—	—	—	Canal Bridge
"	—	—	—	Mintern Street
Mintern Street	—	—	—	Essex Road
Canal Bridge	—	—	—	Angel, Islington
Angel, Islington	—	—	— Cross Street, Upper Street	
Essex Road	—	—	—	Highbury Station
Cross Street, Upper Street	—	—	"	
Highbury Station	—	— Holloway Station, G.N.R.		
Holloway Station, G.N.R.	—	Nag's Head, Holloway		
Nag's Head, Holloway	—	—		Kingsdown Road
Kingsdown Road	—	—		—Archway Tavern
Archway Tavern	—	—	—	Winchester Hotel
	—	—		Hornsey Lane
" "				
Hornsey Lane	—	—	—	Highgate Village

62 Finsbury Pavement, E.C. 2
April, 1917.

A. L. C. FELL,
General Manager.

104. At the corner of Salisbury Road was the fenced off Whittington Stone, supposedly where the young Dick Whittington rested and heard the bells of London summoning him back to the City where he was to become Lord Mayor. The stone survives, although moved a few yards up the hill, but the M class car on service 9 has not been so fortunate.
(D.Jones Coll.)

105. In this 1911 view car 1451 slowly climbs the steepest part of the hill towards the Village. The mass of advert hoardings to the right have long been removed and the space opened up become a car park for The Old Crown public house, seen better in the next view.
(D.Jones Coll.)

106. The cross roads with Dartmouth Park Hill and Hornsey Lane is today a very busy junction, but still completely without any form of traffic control. Not that there was any need for it when traffic was as light as in this view of an M class four-wheeler, with most through traffic preferring the easier climb up the adjacent Archway Road. (D.Jones Coll.)

107. The upper section of the cable hauled tramway consisted of mostly single track with passing loops. Here car 4 enters the single track just beyond "the Bank", the raised roadway to the left. The notice above the drivers canopy gives the fare, one old penny all the way! (D.Jones Coll.)

108. Car 139 waits at the Bisham Gardens stop, before proceeding the last couple of hundred yards to the terminus. The building partly hidden behind the car had been the former car shed for the cable tramway.   (H.B.Priestley)

The Motorman must not under any circumstances leave the car at this terminus, except by arrangement with the Regulator on duty.

A similar procedure must be adopted at Manor House (Green Lanes) and Lavenderhill and Barnet termini.

The slot grip brake is entirely independent of the hand and magnet brakes, and if necessary, may be applied simultaneously at both ends of the car.

It relies for its action on the friction due to the upward and downward thrusts of its two brake blocks upon the special slot rails which are installed on Highgate-hill.

Under no circumstances may a Motorman driving a car on Highgate-hill leave his platform except at the terminus, and then only when the Conductor or a responsible officer is in charge.

Ascending Highgate Hill :—(1) To lower the brake gear into the slot, the car must be brought to rest with the slot brake immediately over the centre of one of the hatchways. The hatchway should then be opened from the fixture in the pavement by means of a point lever.   The main controller handle should then be placed on a spindle which projects from the side of the truck, when a slight turn in the clockwise direction will enable the pawl which holds this to be released and the brake can then be wound down into its correct position. The hatchway must then be closed.

On arrival at Highgate the Motorman must apply the hand brake to hold the car at rest.   If the car is scheduled to turn at the "Archway Tavern," the Motorman will go to the City end of the car, put on his controller handles, apply the magnetic brake to the 7th notch, tighten up and apply hand brake, and instruct the Conductor to release the brake at the Highgate end of the car.

109. Car 141 running as an extra waits for car 137 to clear the single track before proceeding into the narrowest part of the High Street. The position of some of these loops is still visible in 1995 due to different road surfacing being used when the track was removed over fifty years ago. (H .B.Priestley)

110. With knifeboard seating and no decency panels, cable car 10 passes the Angel public house on its journey down to the Archway Tavern. This is the heart of "the Village" which retains its identity today. (D.Jones Coll.)

111. The Angel public house has been rebuilt and renamed "Ye Olde Angel Inn" and workmen put the finishing touches to the turning circle at the new trolleybus terminus. An HR2 type tram with white painted fender and a wartime headlamp blackout mask descends while another waits in the distance to enter the single line. The traction poles and lamp standards also have painted white stripes to aid vision during times of blackout.
(D.W.K.Jones)

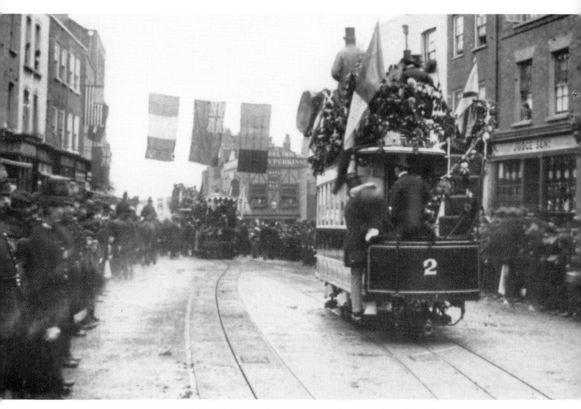

112. This was the scene on the opening day of the cable line, 29th May 1884. Huge crowds, consisting largely of policemen it would appear, turned out to watch the procession of decorated cars. (Hornsey Historical Society)

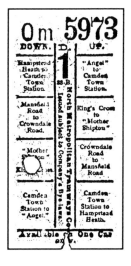

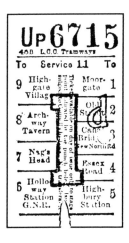

113. The last few yards opened out to double track at the terminus and here car 155 enters the single line to begin the descent of the hill. A lone policeman stands guard by the new trolleybus terminus. (D.Jones Coll.)

Route 11—Conversion to Trolleybus operation

Notice to Inspectors, Drivers and Conductors, Holloway Depot

Commencing on Sunday, 10th December, Route 11 will be converted to trolleybus operation and will be numbered 611.

Fares will be the same as now apply on Route 11 tram. There will be no alterations to existing tickets.

DESTINATION BLINDS

The following wordings must be shewn :—

When Running to	SHOW			
	Front and Rear		Side	
	No.	Wording	No.	Wording
Highgate Village	9	**Highgate Vge.** via New North Road and Highbury	2	Moorgate New North Road Canonbury Road
Moorgate	10	via New North Road and Highbury **Moorgate**		Holloway Road Highgate
Depot	4	**Holloway Depot**	—	——

Lists of wordings of destination and number blinds will be shown in the depot.

114. Car 153 stands at the Highgate Village terminus. Visible through the drivers screen is the handbrake wheel, used for operating the special brakes fitted to these cars for use on the steep hill. To the left is The Gatehouse, a public house built on the site of the former toll gate. (D.Jones Coll.)

115. A final look as passengers leave car 136 while the following traffic waits for them to cross to the pavement. A lone passenger boards car 156 which will be the next to depart for Moorgate. (W.A.Camwell)

6. ROLLING STOCK

Cars 552 - 601. During the latter half of the 1920s the original electric cars of classes A to D had become life expired and were gradually being replaced by the steady arrival of new cars to the Council's standard E/1 design. Coincident with the temporary closure of the Kingsway Subway in February 1930 for reconstruction in order that it could accommodate double deck cars, it had been decided to order a batch of 50 E/1 bodies and to fit them with the trucks and electrical equipment from the withdrawn single deck cars of classes F and G, which had until then worked the Subway services.

As they were withdrawn, the single deck cars were stripped of their equipment at Charlton Works and the bodies were disposed of. The trucks and controllers were then completely overhauled ready for fitting to the new double deck bodies as they were delivered. Although the same fleet numbers were re-used, the second hand equipment did not necessarily go to the new car carrying the same number from which it came. There were reported cases where two cars were carrying the same number at the same time for a short period.

Body construction was based upon the Council's own design of heavyweight steel underframe, on which was mounted the wooden framed lower saloon. Main dimensions were virtually the same as previous E/1s. The addition of a much thicker window pillar at the centre of the lower saloon gave these cars quite a distinctive appearance. Ashanco ventilators were fitted in the space normally occupied by the end quarter lights, which were smaller than usual at half the size of those previously fitted. There was no drivers screen when new. Seating was five rows of upholstered, reversible two and one transverse seats, with a longitudinal triple seat in each corner above the wheel boxes, which also housed the sand hoppers and operating valves.

The upper deck however differed from previous E/1 construction in that the framework was built up from "Alpax" aluminium sections. Other notable differences were in the drop windows, these were now independently opened instead of being connected together and operated by a rack and pinion system. Larger route number stencils were used for the first time, these had become the new standard size for the E/3 and HR2 class cars. Seating was eight rows of two and two upholstered transverse seats, plus seating in the end vestibules for 7. This gave a total capacity of 73 passengers, 27 down and 46 up.

The rebuilt trucks of the maximum traction type had been built by Mountain and Gibson, and were fitted with Westinghouse motors and controllers. At first the cars retained the truck mounted plough carriers, but these were very soon removed, to be fitted directly to the body underframe between the trucks. Wooden framed drivers screens were fitted latterly.

The cars entered service from various depots around the system, but many were allocated to Hampstead Depot where they worked alongside the E class cars on several of the services described in this volume. Following closure of the north side tramways, the 500 series cars were transferred to the southern half of the system where many of them were to be seen working from New Cross Depot covering the 68 and 70 services to London Bridge and Waterloo. Many vehicles survived until the final day of London's Tramways and then they were scrapped. While the bodies were only twenty years old, the trucks had given 46 years of service.

116. One of the original 1883 eight wheel cable trams for the Highgate Hill line is depicted here. (J.H.Price Coll.)

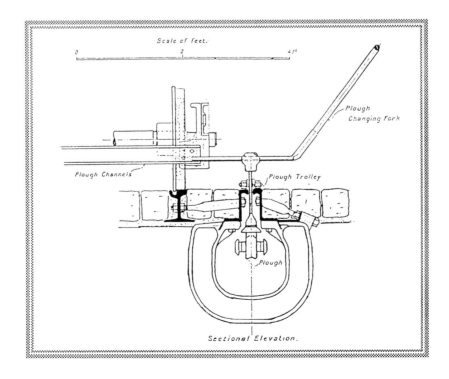

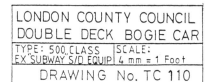

LONDON COUNTY COUNCIL
DOUBLE DECK BOGIE CAR

TYPE: 500, CLASS EX SUBWAY S/D EQUIP	SCALE: 4 mm = 1 Foot
DRAWING No. TC 110	

SCALE
FEET

0   3   6   9   12

7' 2" OVER DRIP RAILS

4

7' 1"

FRONT BRAKE RUNNER BOX

DESTINATION
INDICATOR BOX

584

SHORT YOKE.

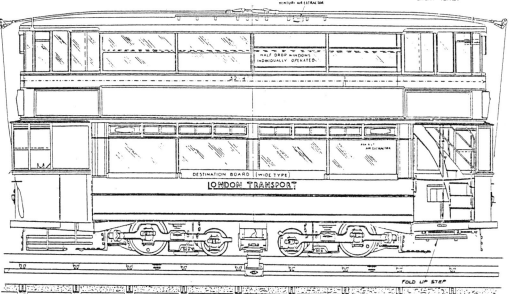

VENTURI AIR EXTRACTOR

HALF DROP WINDOWS
INDIVIDUALLY OPERATED

32. 1

AIR EXTRACTOR

DESTINATION BOARD ((WIDE TYPE)

LONDON TRANSPORT

FOLD UP STEP

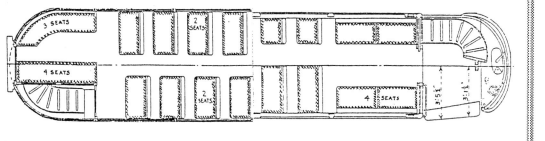

3 SEATS

2 SEATS

4 SEATS

2 SEATS

4 SEATS

117. Car 600 was photographed at the Abbey Wood terminus of service 38. Still in the original LCC livery of red and cream, it carries the LCC crest on the body side. The plough carrier is mounted on the nearest truck. Note that the drop windows on the upper deck have been opened. (R.Elliott)

→

118. An end on view of car 566 on the former Walthamstow service 57 at Chingford Mount. This car has a "Hampstead" type destination box with space for three lines of display. Many cars retained these boxes until the end but with the space for the top line painted over. The fleet number has been changed to the standard style of the new London Transport and a cleat has been added to the dash for tying down the trolley rope. A rear view mirror just visible folded against the staircase is now standard equipment. (A.B.Cross)

119. The upper deck of car 559 is seen on the last day of tramway operation in the capital, 5th July 1952. (J.C.Gillham)

121. Car 577 is caught by the camera at Eltham Green Roundabout on service 44. The advert mouldings have been removed from the upper deck sides, to be replaced by a single moulding running from end to end. The thicker centre window pillar is clearly shown here, as is the folding step, always kept in the up position at the drivers end. Although fitted with double trolleys from new, this car appears to have only one. The body mounted plough carrier is clearly shown in this view. (D.Jones Coll.)

120. The lower deck of car 559 is glimpsed with both bulkhead doors slid open. Note the Last Tram Week poster underneath the fleet number. Further views of this type of tram are included in companion Middleton Press album, *Southwark and Deptford Tramways*. (J.C.Gillham)